From Valleys to Mountains

Susie Piper

authorHOUSE®

AuthorHouse™ LLC
1663 Liberty Drive
Bloomington, IN 47403
www.authorhouse.com
Phone: 1-800-839-8640

Published by AuthorHouse   07/11/2014

ISBN: 978-1-4969-2358-5 (sc)
ISBN: 978-1-4969-2393-6 (e)

Contents

FOREWORD

This book of poetry has been written to tell about beginnings, struggles, poverty, hardships and the up and onward journey of African Americans. This includes times from the days of slavery to emancipation and eventually to the present day status.

This poetic history has been presented in special readings and as dramatizations during Black History Month, at Family Reunions, schools and churches..

The Author

DEDICATION

To my great-granddaughter

Brittany Eula Norris

And

To my great-great granddaughters

Kianna Janee' Johnson
Brianna Williams

Love,

Ma-ma

I AM THE GENERATION

I am the generation

> *of those who long ago*
> *walked in the bonds of slavery*
> *labored in the cotton fields*
> *from the dawn of morn*
> *'til the dusk of the sun*

I am the generation

> *of a generation*
> *of those who shed the shackles of slavery*
> *emerging into a self-realization*
> *of a struggle to survive*
> *the Jim Crow laws, and*
> *longing for the freedom of speech*
> *the right to vote*

I am the generation

> *of a generation*
> *who lived in a segregated world*
> *shackled by the chains of hatred*
> *a survival of the holocaust of lynchings*
> *and denials of a rightful place in*
> *a democratic society*

Susie Piper

I am the generation

> *of generation*
> *whose determination was boosted*
> *with the necessity of changing a way of life*
> *and marching to the cadence of a new drumbeat*
> *into a future filled*
> *with peace, hope and security*

I am the generation

> *of a generation*
> *who aimed for the mountain top*
> *and climbed to the hilltop*
> *but yet amidst the struggles of human frailty*
> *still struggling for a rightful place*
> *hoping…praying…striving,…*
> *for the future generation that is yet to be*

Crayton Reunion 1993

ECHOES OF THE PAST

From the midst of shattered dreams
bleeding hearts and shed tears
from the hopes of those who long ago
dwelt with suffering days and many fears

To belong, to succeed, to make a better place
comes a daring breed who marched in times existing
settling for nothing less than a simple right
a new way to survive was their fight

Looking for the opportunity and a chance
to shine as a beacon light in the night
To become a worthwhile figure in our world to-day
for each, a source of strength, a show of might

No longer a laborer, servant or tiller of soil
or slave, chauffeur, butler or maid
new breeds, doctors, lawyers, politicians
all better pathways for others now laid

Let your reverberations sound over mountain tops,
Let them echo loudly new deeds and new ways,
and make waves for new generations yet to come
so they too, will have better days.

Crayton Legacy-1995

SAGA OF A BLACK WOMAN

Black Woman, Created by God,
Created in bouquets of Ebony, Brown and Ivory hues,
Placed in the enchanted land of Africa,
With its range of strange creatures and views.

Black Woman, Created by God,
Bearing the burdens and cares of the day,
Meeting the challenging facades of life,
Accepting whatever life may display.

Black Woman, Created by God.
Stolen by foreigners from the African shores,
Sold to become slaves to a master's will,
Yet unrelenting, non-complaining
to her suffering and woes.

Black Woman, Created by God,
Carried across oceans to America's new land,
Tossed about in confusion and turmoil,
Suffering the cruelty of a master's hand.

Black Woman Created by God,
Compelled to obey the wiles of man,
A servant, wife, mother; yet still a slave,
And secretly obeying Almighty God's command.

Black Woman Created by God
Rising up from slavery's throng,
Escaping, rejoicing, prayerfully marching
To a new freedom, singing a joyous song

Black Woman Created by God,
Walking, running, achieving new heights,
Searching, seeking for broader roads,
Looking for the brighter lights

Black Woman, Created by God
Arriving at the mountain top
Educator, politician, doctor, lawyer
Singer, actor, - a divinely new crop

Black Woman, Created by God,
With faith in her heart and God by her side
Prayerfully upward and onward she goes,
Awaiting the time that with God she'll abide.

© 1985

THUNDERCLOUDS OF LIFE

Prejudice is the phenomenal thundercloud of the mind
Yet oft hidden from the eyes of mankind
But sometimes appearing like the quills of a porcupine
And emitting the stench of the skunk

Prejudice is evidenced in mannerisms
The sound of the voice tonality
Laced with desires of vengeance
And the walk of superiority

Prejudice is masked in the facial contours
Still bursting forth in torrential downpours
Spreading floods of hatreds in surroundings
Creating fear and uncertainty in the hearts of others

©2009

WE HAVE SURVIVED

Slavery Through War Times

Tossed and driven from the African lands
To a foreign unknown abode as slaves
Families separated…muscular men…beautiful
women and sometimes children
Shackled with chains of slavery
Destined to a new way of life
Field Hand, Male Servant, Concubine
Always to the plantation bidder
Suffering under the throes of hatred
Procrastination, mutilation, lynching,
Promoting a divided nation
Half for servitude and half for justice
We have survived!

Get on board – Trains a-coming
Conducted by brave Harriet Tubman
Destination north! Leaving the Old South!
Seeking, searching, looking for freedom
Freedom to speak; Freedom from hard labor:
Freedom! Freedom! Freedom!
We have survived!

Called by any old name, took it all
Coons, Darkies, Niggers, Negroes
Griffes, Mulattos, Quadroons, Octoroons
Spades, Colored Folk, Africans, Blacks, Boy
Girl, Brothers, African American, Afro-American
Americans of African Descent
Personification through the years
We have survived!

Free at last! Free at last!
Said the Emancipation Proclamation
Free at last, did you say?
Yes, was the answer, but no visibility…
Separate facilities, but supposedly equal
Can't sit here! Can't eat there!
Drink from the colored fountain
Ride in the back of the bus
Go to a school for colored only
With hand-me-down books and
Old coal stove…used ragged uniforms
For your favorite athlete
We have survived!

World War I...World War II...
Korean War...Vietnam War
Been there too…giving our best
Still hoping, yet coping, just waiting
For that better way of life
Civil rights! Rights to vote!
No more separate schools and hand-me-downs
Let me live in any part of town!
Looking to a brighter future
Fair play! Elimination of prejudice!
Dispelling of segregationist ideals
Still searching for the unity of all mankind
We have survived!

'20' Through '40's

We've come a long way
Through the storms of life and rains of woe
Yet struggling from the aftermath of Wars
Still literally shackled in a form of slavery
Can't vote! No money for poll tax
Picking and chopping cotton – 50 cents a hundred pounds
Eating rabbits, 'possums, doves of the wild
We have survived!

Living in those little shot-gun houses
Always located somewhere across the tracks
Bearing the brunt of a separate community
Living in the slums, suburbs, poor section of town
Eating pigs feet, chitterlings, neck bones, greens and beans
Or whatever wasn't wanted by aristocratic folk
Outdoor toilets, tin washtub for bathing
No running water; well water, river water
or water from the tank for all things
We have survived!

Can't eat no food at that Dairy Queen
Buy, but eat on the side of the road
Eat your food in the kitchen of the White Café
'cause Colored folk ain't allowed up front
Depression, starvation, soup line, W. P. A.
Still riding that truck to the cotton field
Still going south to gather that watermelon
Looking for that elusive dollar, to survive
Second hand clothes; save that feed sack
Make a dress, panties or shirt, but still
Isolated, segregated, ostracized, criticized
We have survived!

Still…more wars come; just call those boys!
Put 'em on the front line of all these wars,
But segregate, isolate and criticize them
When they get back to American shores
No more segregation and no more isolation
For those who fought for their country
Fighting for justice for all mankind,
So let justice be done!
Count all mankind as worthy and free!
We have survived!

Walls A-Crumbling

Rise up sister! Stand up brother!
Let your vote count! Let freedom ring!
Let the melodic song of your beautiful voice
Be heard from shore to shore
And vibrate the walls of the smallest home
To the magnificence of the White House
No! you can't sing there! Your voice can't be heard!
Yes! Spoke justice and Eleanor Roosevelt
You shall sing!
The echoes of your voice will vibrate
Through walls where all men walk.
We have survived!

Dare to stand tall, for justice will come forth
Like the rising of the sun
Bursting forth its rays of warmth on a new day
Dare to live tall! Let your integrity and your
Intelligence reflect its beams to future generations
Dare to speak loud!
Echo the spoken word to all mankind.
No more segregation! No more isolation!
No more ostracizing! No more criticizing!
Shout! Free at last! Free at last!
We will survive!

Your gift from God will come forth.
You will write songs that spills forth,
The faithfulness of those who once were
Criticized, ostracized, isolated, and segregated
The melodic tones will forever sound
From generation to generation, and
Spread forth to all nations.
The sweetness of these melodies will open hearts
Hearts of prejudice and hearts of hatred
There will be a new birth, a transformation
Of the minds of those who once shut their eyes
To truth and turned their faces from justice
We have survived!

A New Vision

No more "for colored only" places
No more riding trains behind smoke belching engines
No more "colored only on the old war fronts"
No "private only" but commanders,
Lieutenants and such
No more "closed doors" in the education world
Just a new vision...a new reality... new beginning
We have survived!

The martyrs of the new birth of freedom
Martin Luther King, Jr., Medgar Evers, John
Fitzgerald Kennedy, Ruby Bridges, Rosie Parks,
Malcolm X, Lyndon Baines Johnson fought for
Impartialities, righteousness, truth, and virtue,
Working to close the doors of segregation
To open doors of freedom and opportunity
Seeking, searching for justice to all
We have survived

Yet in the far distance are still doors to be opened,
Freedoms to be sought and fields yet unexplored
Broad fields of to burst forth. and
A legacy left by those who have survived
For generations who have yet to tread
The narrow pathways that spell a new kind of freedom
And a broader vision for all mankind
Yet walking… running…talking…working and
Praying with a special hope
That one day soon, we shall all be one
United together in the sight of God
We shall survive!

Black History 2001

DEDICATION

To all who have experience the trials and tribulations

Prior to the present day, and to those generations who follow in the years to come…..may these history lessons serve as an inspiration to all who hope to keep the dream alive.

The theme "The Color Line Revisited: Is Racism dead?" was chosen for February 2002. When we take a look at a divisional time of racial issues, can we safely say that the color live is being revisited, or can one safely say that the color line yet remains as an invisible line of demarcation, waiting to be diminished by future generations.

A glance into the capsule of time lets us know, that much has been accomplished, but there is still a long ways to go. This dates from 1920 to the present time.

The Author

"Retrospect"

God looked upon His beautiful world,
At His creatures who were in bondage,
He said: "No more! No more!
No More suffering from cruelty and rage.

So North and South engaged in war,
A Civil War, they called it.
South said: "Oh yes! Slaves we'll have."
But North replied: "No, No! 'Tis just unfit.

Many lives were lost, but slaves were freed,
In the war of wars….this Civil War
Some went north and some went south
Their lives were scarred and scattered far.

20 acres and a mule were promised,
But did this dream come true?
Freedmen lived on, in plantation style,
And simply tried to endure

A spot for a little vegetable garden
Perhaps a hog, cow, and chicken or two,
Hand-me-down clothes and a shuck bed,
These families just made things do!
Out in the nowhere, down on the farm
Wide open spaces, and muddy dirt roads,
Folks stayed together on one accord
Brave ancestors carried these heavy loads

II

Twenties and Thirties

World War I ends and triumphant armies of khaki clad Negro soldiers passed in review down New York's fifth Avenue to the cheers of thousands of happy citizens. And yet, so very soon, after the victory parades ended, these same soldiers all over the country, big cities and small towns, were forced to defend their very lives.

There was a fearful wave of lynchings, beatings in the street and unfair treatment, because of the fear of these soldiers demanding fair treatment. Most had returned, only to have to return to the farms as a tenant or sharecropper farmer.

In spite of all these things, great leaders emerged. Carter G. Woodson, founder of Negro History Week; Marcus Garvey, who directly attacked racism and encouraged Black business enterprises; folklorist and early novelist, Zora Neale Hurston; Madam C. J. Walker, the first Black Woman millionaire; Mary McCleod Bethune, founder of Bethune-Cookman College; and the NAACP became prominent in fighting for justice.

The great depression brought some changes, for Franklin Delano Roosevelt, one of America's greatest presidents, came forth with his New Deal program, and along with his wife, Eleanor, began looking into the plight of the Black Man. These were the uncertain and unstable twenties and thirties.*

"'20's and '30's"

Then came the twenties and thirties
A new way of living seemed to arrive
Tenant farmers, sharecroppers, cooks, janitors,
Chop cotton! Pick Cotton! Pull Corn!
Bale Hay! Just to stay alive
Been There!... Done That Too!

Saturday was a special day for all of the family.
Going to town, buying groceries for folk to eat,
Want a hamburger? Go to the café, not up front,
But kitchen back…
Sat in a corner at that table and make shift seat
Been There!...Done That Too!

Needed some shoes…can't try them on…
Need a Sunday hat! No! No! you can't try that!
Your hair ain't right, but buy if you want it
Besides, you must think you are some aristocrat!
Been There! Done That too!

Family went to church on Sunday morn
Spent the day in the House of God
Children sat up front on the very first bench
With their behavior controlled by Mom with a nod.
Been There! Done That Too!

Went to the all Black School
Heated by a coal burning pot-bellied stove
No janitor? No! Students did the chores…
Studied hand-me-downs, outdated, used books in the alcove
Been There! Done That Too!

***

"To everything there is a season,
and a time to every purpose under the heaven,
a time to cast away stones, and a
time to gather stones together;
a time to embrace,
and a time to refrain from embracing.
Ecclesiastes 3: 1-5
KJV

III

'30's and '40's"

The forties and fifties were a brand new era
Big bands, famous songbirds began to sing.
Time was marching on and time does change
Folk were getting tired of the same old thing,
Been There….Done That Too!

World War II, then the Korean battle came
And men on the front were losing their life
New thoughts came to mind; new visions foreseen
Our boys stood tall, and became martyrs of strife
Been There…Done That Too!

No more beatings! No more lynching!
'Twas the cry throughout the land
No more back doors! No more separate schools!
Crossed the mind of every man
Been There …Done that too!

It's time for all mankind to be as one
And peaceful ventures to pursue
It's time to fight for things deserved
To stand tall, pray united,
Although suffering may endure
Been There…Done That Too!

***

"Wisdom, like an inheritance is a good thing,
And benefits those who see the sun.
Wisdom is a shelter as money is a shelter,
But the advantage of knowledge is this,
That wisdom preserves the life of its possessor."
Ecclesiastes &:11-12
KJV

IV

The Sixties Thru' Two Thousand Two

The Sixties emerged, and the Civil Rights battle was in full blast, not a battle of using ammunition, but many battles…sit-ins, mass marching, eloquent words encouraging non-violence, boycotts, etc. Every Congress of Racial Equality (CORE) member carried a card which read:

Don't strike back or curse if abused.
Don't laugh out
Don't block entrances to the stores or the aisles.
Show yourself friendly and courteous at all times.
Remember love and non-violence.
May God bless you.

1963 often called the "Year of Decision," was another year of unrest. It was the 100th Anniversary of the Emancipation Proclamation. It was the beginning of many marches and speeches by Dr. Martin Luther King. It was the year he wrote "We Can't Wait." 3000 people in Birmingham, Alabama went to jail. Dogs and fire hoses were used, and many Whites who believed in justice suffered the same cruelties as Blacks.

President Kennedy told the nation: "Our people will not be fully free, until all of its citizens are free."

To dramatize the demands for equality to the nation, the largest protest in America took place on August 28, 1963. On that day, buses, trains, cars, and planes brought Washington, D. C. its greatest crowd in history, a quarter of a million people. And on that day, the most famous speech ever delivered in America was spoken by Dr. Martin Luther King; "I Have A Dream."

This gigantic event reached the four corners of the world. However, it did not conclude on that day, for there were many other marches, murders and senseless crimes that occurred, but the Black Revolution was in, and to Black citizens, there was no turning back.

Congress responded to the Civil Rights crusades with stronger laws in 1964 and 1956. The 1964 law aimed to eliminate segregation and discrimination in broad areas of American life!

Employment, education, public accommodations and voting rights were changed. The 24th Amendment to the Constitution eliminated poll tax in federal elections, and the 1965 Civil Rights Law eliminated literacy tests and other devices which prevented Blacks from voting.

One cannot relate in a short time, all of the things that have happened since the sixties…the assassinations of one of America's greatest presidents, John F. Kennedy and non-violent leader, Martin Luther King…the many arrests in major cities…the changes brought about due to the Vietnam war…the prison riots of the '70's, the Desert Storm Wars, and today's War on Terrorism in Afghanistan.*

Yet we can be thankful for the progress that has been made. We must still continue to strive for recognition, not for color changes, but for innate abilities and qualifications. United We Stand!

*Excerpts from "Eye Witness: The Negro in American History By: William Loren Katz – 3rd Edition 1974

"60's Thru' 2002"

God used ordinary people
People like you and me
People with zeal and foresight
Who fought to set us free
Been There! Done That Too!

God used ordinary people
During the years of integration
Civil Right Laws, Freedom Marches for mankind
Was the battle cry of our United Nation
Been there! Done That Too!

Remember the 60's, 70's and the 80's
The 90's and a new century too.
Progress was made and much has been done
But still, there remains so much to do
Been there! Done That Too!

So those of us who traveled these roads,
And for those who stood the test,
Pass on the torch to future generations
Tell them to strive, work and do their best.
Been there! Done that too!
****

"I will praise you, O Lord with all my heart.
I will tell of all your wonders.
I will be glad and rejoice to you.
I will sing praises to you, O most high…
"Sing praises to the Lord, enthroned in Zion;
proclaim among the nations what He has done."
Psalm 9:1-2,12
KJV

Black History 2002

THAT OLD TIME RELIGION

I

Down yonder, under that old branch arbor
Or maybe in that one room church
Folk didn't have no fancy seats
They just couldn't afford very much

The one thing they had was faith in God
And a whole lot of genuine love
Love for one another and love for God
Who came down from heaven above.

II

Children, this is Saturday morn
And you don't have to go to school
So just get right out of that bed
You know! You must abide by the family rule.

Get that left over biscuit on that plate
And put a shine on your high top shoes
Wash and iron your Sunday best
So we can go listen to God's good news.

We're going to cook that Sunday meal
Maybe some fried chicken, a cake and a pie
You know, we don't do no work on God's day
No matter how hard we may try

Fold up that baby's quilt right now
You know he will need a little nap
We gotta' listen to the preached Word
And I don't want the baby in my lap

III

Now let's go down to that old branch arbor
And lift our voices in song
When we get done a singing and praying
The Reverend will teach us how to do no wrong

Pray for your neighbors
And pray for your friends
Pray for your enemies
God's blessings don't have no end

You say, "we ain't got no piano nor organ"
Think now! You got a voice, hands and feet.
God has given you the rhythm in your bodies
So come on church, and let's have a great meet

IV
BLUEGRASS PRAISES

Bluegrass music started long, long ago
With people from a foreign land
They came to America in 1600
And formed a musical band

Carolinas, Tennessee,Virginia, Kentucky
Became new homes for a new kind of song
They wrote songs of happenings from each day
Reflecting good times, hard times, right and wrong

First, they called it mountain music
As it spread throughout the south
From this, the country music soon evolved
Good and happy words came from their mouth

Sing a song of traditions
A song of trials and mirth
Sing your music for all to embrace
Let it ring throughout God's earth.

Black History ©2005

WE ARE THE PEOPLE

I

We are the people
who landed on American shores
shackled with chains
placed into slavery'
tilled the soil
tended the Master's families
toiled by the daylight'
ran at twilight

We are the people
who faced the divisions of life
sometimes loved and often hated
sometimes jailed and even lynched
but walked and ran on
struggled through Jim Crowism
strived hard to survive
here....there...everywhere
We are the people!

We are the people
who attended segregated schools
ate in back door kitchens
drank from separate fountains
sat in the back of the bus
fought in American battles
yet ostracized, criticized, minimized
but still without hope
for a new kind of freedom
We are the people!

II

We are the people
who sought justification and vindication
opened doors, impartialities
truth, virtue, for all mankind
yet lived with joy and inner peace

We are the people
who have survived
the bonds of slavery
the Jim Crow laws
the boundaries of segregation
marching to the cadence
of a new drumbeat
unlocking doors of new opportunities

We are the people
teachers, lawyers, doctors
engineers, actors, counselors
secretaries, dieticians, soldiers
We are survivors
yet fighting for unseen justice
in a modern world
hoping for a miraculous future
of love, hope, peace, forevermore

III

We are the people
the leaders of yesterday
echoes of the past
yet dreamers of a new day
building new legends
introducing future journeys
for times to come
and times to be

We are the people
the founders of yesterday
opening doors of opportunities
laying foundations for tomorrow
the spokesman for political justice
paving roads of new freedom
a generation of perseverance
role models bearing the crosses

We are the people
those who paved the way
martyrs of yesterday
assassinated for just causes
but still pressing forward
to a better way of life
in the land of the free
and the home of the brave

IV

We are the people!
those of the present generation
born of our forefathers
ancestors of oblivion
without necessities of life
struggling to succeed

We are the people
with no profound backgrounds for learning
using hand-me-down books
attending church supported colleges
determined to succeed
to reach a designated goal in life

We are the people
the caregivers, nurses, midwives
servants of many tasks
tending the needs of the rich and the poor
educators, teaching and achieving
a measure of success in a segregated world

We are the people!
doctors healing the lame, sick, poor and rich
lawyers providing justice in a cruel world
soldiers on war torn battlefields
community activists…spokesmen for necessities
yes, we have made it, but must continue
to provide a future for others to lead

V

We are the people!
those who have overcome
those who have survived
succeeding in spite of
traveling narrow pathways
crossing fences of injustice

We are the people!
yesterdays' dreams
hopes of tomorrow
moving onward and upward
venturing into a new day
opening those closed doors
tearing down brick walls
fulfilling those hopes, those dreams
for generations to follow

VI

We are the new generation
survivors of our forefathers
who taught lessons of life
to prepare us for our future to come
We are the tomorrow
products of our yesterday
building our dreams
learning new skills
We are the people!

Black History 2007

TIME FRAME : 1927 – 1940

INTRODUCTION

We are free…..but yet not free!
We lived…but barely lived.
We often wore tattered clothes to protect our bodies.
We ate distasteful light bread and
tainted meat just to survive.
We were constantly on the move, never
knowing what the next day will bring.
Our families were often victims of
brutality…..rape, and lynchings.
We were befriended by a Quaker family who helped to
educate us, and give us some abilities to read and write.
Yes! We were free, but not free. We had
*hard times, but we survived.**
*The above contains excerpts from a letter written after
slavery ended by a relative of Sister Ilinda Williams,
and contributed for this years' Black History Month.

I

EARLY HARD TIMES

There's a road once traveled,
'Twas some eighty years ago
Hard times was life's highway
For there was much suffering and woe

There were days when times were hard,
And folks worked hard to survive
Toiled the land, all the day long,
Trying hard, just to stay alive.

Chopped cotton, picked cotton…row by row
Pulled corn,… bailed hay, cut maize,… all by hand
Rode plows and cultivators, drawn by mules,
Work, Work…tenant farmer,
sharecropper…white man's land

Drank cool water from the wooden keg,
Ate Bologna sausage and crackers, you see
Time-out came at the midday hour
Rested under the wagon or a nearby tree.

Then comes the end of a worker's day, at sundown,
Folks went home to their 3-room shack.
Time for a bath in that number 3 tub,
Then a late-afternoon meal or snack

Folks didn't have no fancy clothes,
Nor select furniture or "auto-mo-biles",
But they all possessed a spirit of love,
And a great desire to perform God's Will

As they readied themselves for a good night of rest,
They'd sit in an old cane chair.
And read God's Word by a dim oil lamp
His divine words of wisdom to share.

Saturdays finally came around,
Gotta 'wash, iron, and cook Sunday's meal
'Cause Sunday's a special day for all,
for we've got to go and worship God; that's real!

Everybody went to the House of God.
Spent the entire day singing praises on high,
On the Mourners bench or on bended knee,
Praying for better times to come, by and by.

In spite of all the troubles, heartaches and woe,
People walked on with a spirit of love.
Starvations, beatings,lynchings and such,
Were borne with help from above.

There's a road once traveled some eighty years back
Filled with hard times, hard trials and real pain
But it was trod with the vision of much better days,
And promises from on high were to gain.

Could you walk down that road of back then
Place your feet where those older saints trod?
For you'd come to know, how they now walk in peace
Tis only with the help of our sweet God

II
NEW BEGINNINGS – 1941

Folks are still laboring hard in those cotton fields
Yet dancing with joy to the new "big bands."
Wearing penny loafer shoes and the long "zoot" suits
Doing their own thing, yet living off the land

The Japanese bombed Pearl Harbor one cold December morn,
And World War II began. Our boys were
called to task by our beloved country
To fight many battles in foreign lands

Fighting the same fight, yet separated by color,
And often denied the same equal rights.
They represented their country bravely,
In the midst of trials, tribulations and strife.

And at the war's end, our boys came home,
With the light of new found hope in their eyes
Only to be faced the same tales of hatred
And the same horror stories and lies

They had given their all in their fight for our land
Leaving all their loved ones behind
Yet how hard it must have been, when on their return
To find America's people had not changed their minds

III
CHANGING TIMES

Then came the generation of the baby boomers,
A new found quest for civil rights was born
No more back doors and no more separate schools
Voiced the tired, the weary, and the worn

The Vietnam War brought forth a new crisis
With times that tried the souls of Man
And Civil Rights wars fought on the home front
Brought troubles throughout the whole land

A chaotic war of freedom began (waged
from sea to shining sea)
People were beaten, hung, whipped and jailed
Crosses were burned and Blacks marched
They chanted and suffered, yet prevailed

Even more wars and battles, our country's endured,
Desert Shield, Desert Storm, and Iraq
But unity was born from our gain and our pain,
It seems we're finally on the right track

IV
THE PRESENT

Through all of the heartaches, the suffering and pain
Our people just kept marching on
Past assassinations, desegregation, discriminations and more
They stood tall, even when the day was gone

People never lost hope, though days were hard
As great men marched side by side
Singing old hymns, "We Shall Overcome"
And "In Thee, we shall abide!"

A new day has sprung for all of mankind,
New dreams, new times, for all man
Some cry out "There's A Place Called Hope"
And others say "Change… Yes We can!"

Yet through all our dark days, our Father's been faithful
For He never has left us alone
He's with us at all times, thru good times and bad
And even when all hope is gone

Black History 2008

THE QUEST FOR CITIZENSHIP

I

SURVIVAL

Captivity – Slavery – Isolation

Oppression – Suppression – Depression

We have survived!

Racism – Ostracism – Criticism

Beatings – Floggings – Lynchings

We have survived!

Frustrated – Differentiated – Eliminated

Denied – Misinterpreted – Segregated

We have survived!

Sufferings – Humiliations – Desecrations

Imprisoned – Mistaken – Tribulations

We have survived!

II

THE QUEST

The newly freed slaves cried out…

Free at last! Free at last!

Yet the promise of freedom was surfaced portrayed

For the tide of racism seem to spread forth

Like the incontrollable tides of ocean waters

That could not be controlled!

The South cried out: "No! you cannot vote.

A special tax must be paid

Segregation was rampart…

Spreading like the massive forest fires

Beatings, lynchings, all forms of discrimination

Seemed to be the order of the day

But freed man cried out…

We will survive!

III
THE REALITY

"Out of many, we are one."- President Obama

From the bonds of slavery

To a state of freedom

From the back door of life

To the front door of acceptance

From the back of the bus

To the front of the bus

From the segregated schools

To the integrated schools

From the cotton fields and kitchens

To the corporate and business world

From the state of inequality

To the breath of equality

From the color of the skin

To the contents of the character

From the outhouse of long ago

To the White House of America

Yes! Out of many

We have become one

Black History 2009

THE HISTORY OF BLACK ECONOMIC EMPOWERMENT

The theme for Black History Month 2010 is "The History of Black Economic Empowerment. The need for economic development has been a central element of black life. After centuries of unrequited toil as slaves, African Americans gained their freedom and found themselves in the struggle to make a living. The chains were gone, but racism was everywhere. Black codes often prevented blacks from owning land in towns and cities, and in the countryside, they were often denied the opportunity to purchase land. Organized labor shut their doors to their brethren, and even the white philanthropist who funded black schools denied them employment opportunities once educated.. In the South, whites sought to insure that blacks would only be sharecroppers and day labors, and in the North, whites sought to keep them unskilled laborers.

I

The Slavery Economy Empowerment

Gotta' go to the cotton field today
To work for the Master, so I'll have a little pay
Payday was not necessarily money
Believe you me,… this was not funny

Old Massa' gave me a little spot of land
He said: "Plant you a garden, Brother Man
So your children can have some food to eat
Don't let weeds grow in it, ..keep it nice and neat.

Then came pronouncement from Washington, D. C.
Let slaves in the South live to be free
So these freedmen traveled to and fro'
Some just did not know where to go

Twenty acres and a mule would be granted for sure
To help freed people, their hardships to endure
But things were just not better for some of the people
Cause discrimination arose like the tallest steeple.

II

JIM CROW ECONOMIC EMPOWERMENT

Pushing against the odds, African Americans became landowners, skilled workers, small businessmen and women, professionals and ministers. In the Jim Crow economy, they started insurance companies, vocational schools, teachers colleges, cosmetic firms, banks, newspapers, and hospitals.

To fight exclusion from the economy, they started their own unions and professional associations. In an age in which individuals proved unable to counter industrialization alone, they preached racial or collective uplift rather than individual self-reliance. The late nineteenth and early twentieth centuries witnessed an unprecedented degree of racial solidarity and organization...

In 1910, a group of dedicated reformers, black and white, gathered to create an organization to address the needs of African Americans as they migrated to the cities of the United States. The organization that they created a century ago became what we all know as the National Urban League.

For a century, they have struggled to open the doors of opportunity for successive generations, engaging the challenges of each age.

II

THE JIM CROW ECONOMIC EMPOWERMENT

Life in the twenties, thirties and forties was no better
Still in the cotton fields, 'midst toils and fetters
The New Deal economy to help the poor
Tried to relieve suffering, worry and more

Then came forth the great migration
Families moved from all 'cross the nation
World War two was soon declared
Yet lives of people were still greatly impaired

Segregation was rampart for the world to see
Unequal wages, segregated schools for those who were free
Soldiers fought in front lines on the battlefields
Yet returned to their homes; lives unfulfilled.

Through it t all, we still survive
New race solidarity kept us alive.
New ways of dealing, new hopes and new dreams
Brought better living, successes and esteem

BLACK EMPOWERMENT IN AUSTIN

Pushing against the odds, African Americans became successful. Many entered into the world of professionalism. They started their own schools, businesses, colleges, banks, and more, to fight exclusion from the economy.

Let us take a peek into a time capsule for the City of Austin at the turn of the century. The area now known as the entertainment center of Austin, East 6th Street, was a bustling hub of Black owned businesses and establishments. The majority of these enterprises extended up to 6th and Brazos.

There were more than 150 small businesses in the area at one time. It housed all Black entertainment centers, Mr. Timmons Barbershop, and Dr. Hammond's Dental office. I-35 was then known as East Avenue, and was the location of such establishments as Samuel Huston College, the Lookout Hill, better known as Adams Apple, the Shanks Worm Farm, and nearby on 10th St., Ebenezer Baptist Church.

In 1928, the city devised a master plan designed to relocate the city's "*colored folks*" to areas east of downtown. An unintended side effect of that effort was a centralization of the music scene. The Jazz and Blues clubs that originated in East Austin during this time, helped develop the music scene for which Austin is famous for to-day.

Eleventh and Twelfth Streets were designated as the "*Chitterling Circuit*" in the late 20's to the late 60's. 12th Street was the site of many businesses. There was the East

End Barber Shop, the Harlem Theatre, Yates Drugstore, at least six or more nightclubs, a cab stand, hotel and shoe repair store. Sam's Barbecue and Hunt's Real Estate still remain today.

11ᵗʰ Street had 8 night clubs, two cab stands, Christians Beauty School, Atlanta Life Insurance Company, Margie's Barbershop, Southern Dinette, the Elks Lodge, Dr. Young's Pharmacy, Deluxe Hotel and the YWCA. The Victory Grill, where many famous bands and orchestras once performed, still stands as a historical marker in Austin.

The club venues were not the only things that kept early Austinites tapping their feet and clapping their hands. Gospel music was very much alive and vibrant thanks to the efforts of musicians such as Ruth Davis, Rosalie Watrous Wicks, Virgie Carrington DeWitty, The Federation of Choirs, and great songs such as *"Look Where The Lord has Brought Us," "Magnify the Lord", "O, Children"* which incidentally, were composed by Mrs. DeWitty.

It was during this period of time when St. James Missionary Baptist Church was born. It all began in 1927 at 1102 Midway. The history of this religious institution is now 83 years old, and the ancestors of the founders now keep the legacy alive.. *

Note: The above information was contributed by many members of St. James Missionary Baptist Church, most of whom have resided in the City of Austin for a life time.

III

MODERN DAY ECONOMIC EMPOWERMENT

It has been more than 50 years ago
When our people suffered misery and woe.
Yet changes have come in every way
And progress has been made, day by day.

No more cotton fields and back door places
Segregated schools and forbidden spaces.
No more cursing, spittings or illicit names
The hateful experiences began to wane.

We have slowly passed the test,
We've even proved, we are the best.
Now we live in a corporate domain
Seeking to find wealth, fortune and fame.

As we continue on the road of life
We must always remember the heartaches and strife.
Yesterday's gone, yet tomorrow will come
We must continue to fight
'Till victory is won!

WHERE DO WE GO FROM HERE?

In the days of yore… so long ago
Our forefathers came to this land
They were shackled in chain and so downcast
Just afraid to take a Godly stand.

They stole away to the hidden woods
Or down by the old mill stream
To whisper a prayer to the Father above
With hopes of fulfilling a dream.

A dream of freedom and security
A hope for better days to come
A place to lay their weary head
One they could truly call a home.

Where do we go from here?
How long must we suffer woe?
Deliver us, O God, we pray
From struggles in life we undergo.

IDENTITY

Girl…. Adult Black Woman

Boy…Adult Black Man

Nigger…All people of African descent

Negroes… Specified Classification

Blacks… New race definition

Afro Americans…New faces

African American… Newest Identity

An American of African descent

Who am I?

FANGS OF PREJUDICE

The predator lies in wait
like the coral snake or the feared cobra.
And like the feared reptiles
lashes his tongue in a vicious manner.
The prejudiced person stands in view ..coyly,
swaying to and fro in a friendly manner,
awaiting to strike his poisonous tongue at a
victim' with spoken words or ostracism.
The spoken word used to poke fun, or slyly
insinuating a lack of knowledge,
misunderstanding, intelligence or just to degrade
his victim with the fangs of prejudice
The victim experiencing years of pain and degradation,
mind experimentations, rude awakenings, sits
quietly in moments of meditation,. Yet assured
within, that this too, one day shall pass.
The fangs of prejudice lash out in many ways
regardless of race, creed, or color.
Its venomous words hurt but for a moment,
and are soon passed away in the midst of the mind.
The prejudicial person becomes like a mist,
appearing to cloud the minds of those who are near.
Ne'er realizing…they too, shall disappear someday
and the sun will appear to warm the heart of the victim.

UNITY

Way back when
Mama cooked the Sunday meal on Saturday
Packed it in a basket to take to church on Sunday
Papa fixed the wagon up on Saturdays
Dressed down the mules early Sunday morn
The whole family loaded up in the wagon
Packed those quilts and blankets for the babies
To nap on a pallet while church service was held
The afternoon meal was spread on the grounds
All shared the food that was prepared
Readying for an afternoon time of worship
Children sat erect on the front pew
Conduct was a must…
Good behavior or face a willow switch
Everybody sang together in tune or out of tune
The preacher and his family were your family too
Everybody cared and shared burdens
Trials and tribulations
Unity

THOUGHTS ON PREJUDICE

PREJUDICE

> *mirrored reflections of hatred*
> *enveloping the soul of mankind holding the mind in captivity*
> *allowing him to walk in the darkness*
> *yet seeing and yet not seeing*
> *unable to accept the creation*
> *of the White, the Brown, the Black of the White, the Brown, the Black*

PREJUDICE

> *catechism of spoken and unspoken words*
> *harsh in nature, cutting, cutting like a mighty sword*
> *name calling, blasphemy, viciously*
> *emerging forth like hot lava from a volcano*
> *destroying desires and virtues*
> *dispelling cacophony and provocations*
> *spreading over the White, the Brown, the Black*

PREJUDICE

> *destruction of soul within*
> *and beauty without*
> *forces of evil grasping each mind*
> *cold-hearted, unrelenting in constancy*
> *swirling like tornado winds*
> *vicious and uncaring in destruction*
> *reflected in the countenance*
> *of the White, the Brown, the Black*

PREJUDICE

> *thoughts of mankind*
> *expressions of inward and outward feelings*
> *taught concepts from out of the past*
> *inhibited and uninhibited rituals*
> *passed down from generation to generation*
> *unyielding, sacrificial, greed, dishonesty*
> *brutality, unwarranted behavior, self-destruction found in*
> *the White, the Brown, the Black*

PREJUDICE

ABOUT THE AUTHOR

   Susie E. Moultry Sansom-Piper was born in Milam County, in the City of Rockdale, Texas. She graduated from Aycock High School in 1937 as Salutatorian of her class.

She received an Associate Degree in Business Administration from St. Phillips Junior College of San Antonio, Texas; graduating with second honors.

She graduated Magna Cum Laude from Samuel Huston College (now Huston Tillotson University) of Austin, Texas, with a Bachelor of Science degree in Business Administration. A Master's Degree in Administration and Elementary Education, with Honors, was conferred upon her from Prairie View University. She also completed Counselor Certification from Prairie View University. Additional Studies were completed in Mathematics and Chemistry under the National Science Foundation Program conducted by the U.S. Government.

She taught in the Rockdale Public School system for Rockdale, Texas, for a total of 41 years. For 23 years, she taught at Aycock, the school for Blacks, serving as the last school principal and also "bridging the gap" of integration. The following 17 years were spent in the Junior High School as an instructor of Texas History.

In addition to a teaching career, she is a free-lance writer to the Rockdale Reporter. She has featured such writings as "Way Back When", 28 years of "Ebony Etchings", "Aycock Nostalgia", and "On The Other Side of The Tracks." She has written "The Purple Tiger" -- The History of Aycock High School, and "Tied To Mama's Apron Strings."

She has received many poetry awards, authored four inspirational pamphlets, and is currently editor of the "Reflections", her church newsletter. She also serves as musician for the *Goldenaires*, a choir featuring Senior Citizens.

After retirement, she visited many schools, government organizations and nursing homes, giving illustrations and stories that were featured in "Way Back When."

One of her favorite statements is: "I retired from the classroom to go to work on something else." She further states: "It has been a great pleasure and unspeakable joy, not only to have touched the lives of many students, but to have the opportunity to relive the memory of a great, great school."